A Celebration of Memories
A Record Book

ISBN 1-57977-145-9

Made in China

Published by Havoc Publishing
San Diego, California

Artwork by Laurie Korsgaden

Please write to us for more information
on Havoc Publishing products.

Havoc Publishing
9808 Waples Street
San Diego, California 92121

This book belongs to:

This is a record of all of my favorite memories.
These special keepsakes, photographs and recorded
thoughts make this book unique and special.

Contents

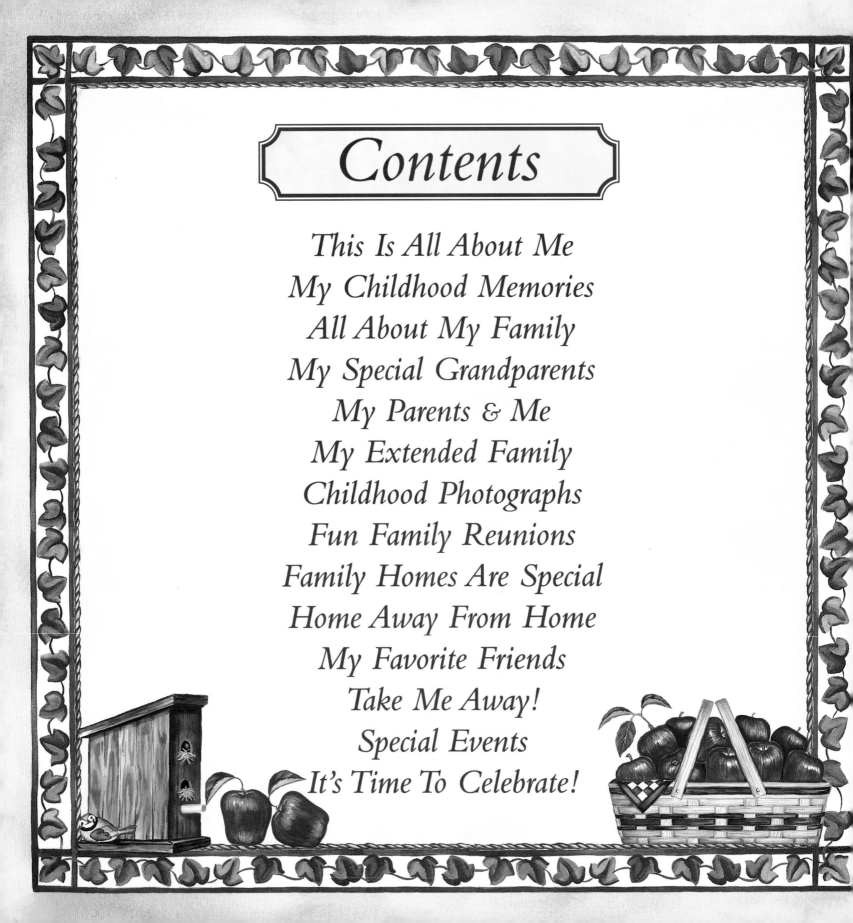

Contents

This Is All About Me

The memories that I cherish the most are about:_____

_____

_____

_____

_____

_____

_____

This is a list of things I own that hold special memories for me:_____

_____

_____

_____

_____

_____

_____

_____

The qualities I like most about myself are: _____

_____

_____

_____

_____

When I am alone with myself, I daydream about: _____

_____

_____

_____

_____

My favorite memories of places I've been are: _____

_____

_____

_____

_____

My Childhood Memories

My favorite memories about growing up are: _____

_____

_____

_____

_____

_____

_____

My favorite childhood playmates were:

_____

_____

_____

Laurie Korsgaden

While I was growing up, I attended school at: _____

_____

_____

_____

_____

In school, my favorite teachers, classmates and activities were: _____

_____

_____

All About My Family

My favorite memories of special times spent with my family are: _____

_____

_____

_____

_____

_____

_____

My favorite family story is about: _____

_____

_____

_____

_____

_____

_____

_____

_____

_____

Family Photograph

My Special Grandparents

My favorite memories of times spent with my grandparents are: _____

_____

_____

_____

_____

_____

_____

Some special things that I have learned from my grandparents are: _____

_____

_____

_____

_____

_____

_____

_____

_____

My Parents & Me

My parents are very special people because: _____

_____

_____

_____

_____

My favorite memories about growing up with my parents are: _____

_____

_____

_____

_____

My favorite memories of quality times spent with my parents are: _____

_____

_____

_____

_____

_____

These are a few things that my parents have taught me: _____

_____

_____

_____

_____

My Extended Family

These are wonderful memories about my aunts and uncles: _____

_____

_____

_____

_____

_____

My favorite story about my cousins and me: _____

_____

_____

_____

_____

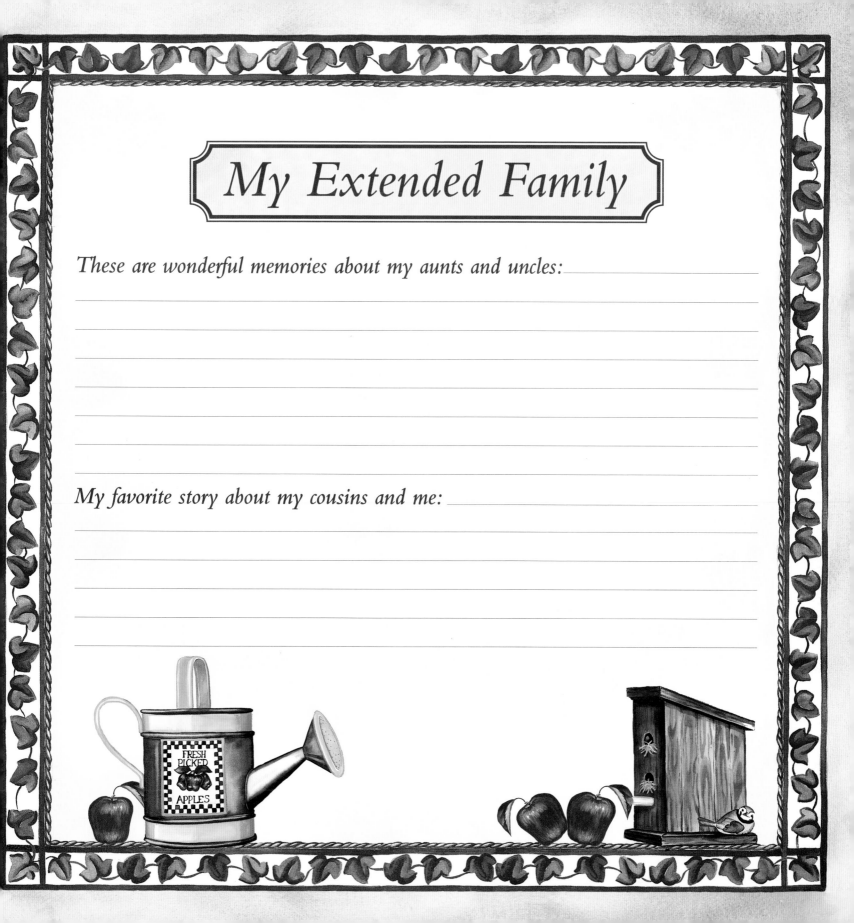

Childhood Photographs

Childhood Photographs

Fun Family Reunions

The best family reunions have been spent with: _____

_____

_____

_____

_____

_____

_____

_____

The locations where the family all gathered were: _____

_____

_____

Special memories about the reunions are: _____

_____

_____

_____

_____

Family Photograph

Family Homes Are Special

While growing up, my favorite house that we lived in was: _____

_____

_____

_____

_____

_____

_____

My favorite neighbors were: _____

_____

_____

_____

_____

_____

_____

The family pets I had growing up were: _____

_____

_____

_____

_____

Pets are part of the family

HOME

This is a story about when I first moved away from home: _____

_____

_____

_____

_____

_____

_____

The address of my new place was: _____

_____

_____

Here is a description of what it looked like: _____

_____

_____

_____

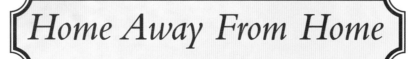

Home Away From Home

This is a story about me and my roommates: _____

_____

_____

_____

_____

_____

Here are some stories about living on my own: _____

_____

_____

_____

_____

_____

_____

My Favorite Friends

My best friends who have touched my life are: _____

_____

_____

_____

This is a little history about these friendships: _____

_____

_____

_____

_____

_____

Take Me Away!

My favorite local vacation spots are: _____

_____

_____

_____

_____

_____

_____

Someday I would like to visit these places: _____

_____

_____

_____

_____

_____

_____

The most romantic places that I have visited are: _____
_____
_____
_____

My favorite historical places that I remember visiting are: _____
_____
_____
_____

My favorite island getaway that I dream about is: _____
_____
_____
_____

Some of the places that I would like to visit again are: _____
_____
_____
_____

Special Events

Some of my favorite musicals and plays are: _____

_____

_____

_____

_____

_____

_____

These are some of the special trips that I've made to the theater, museums and exhibits:

_____

_____

_____

_____

_____

It's Time To Celebrate!

Some of my favorite birthdays have been spent with:

Some special engagements and weddings that I remember are:

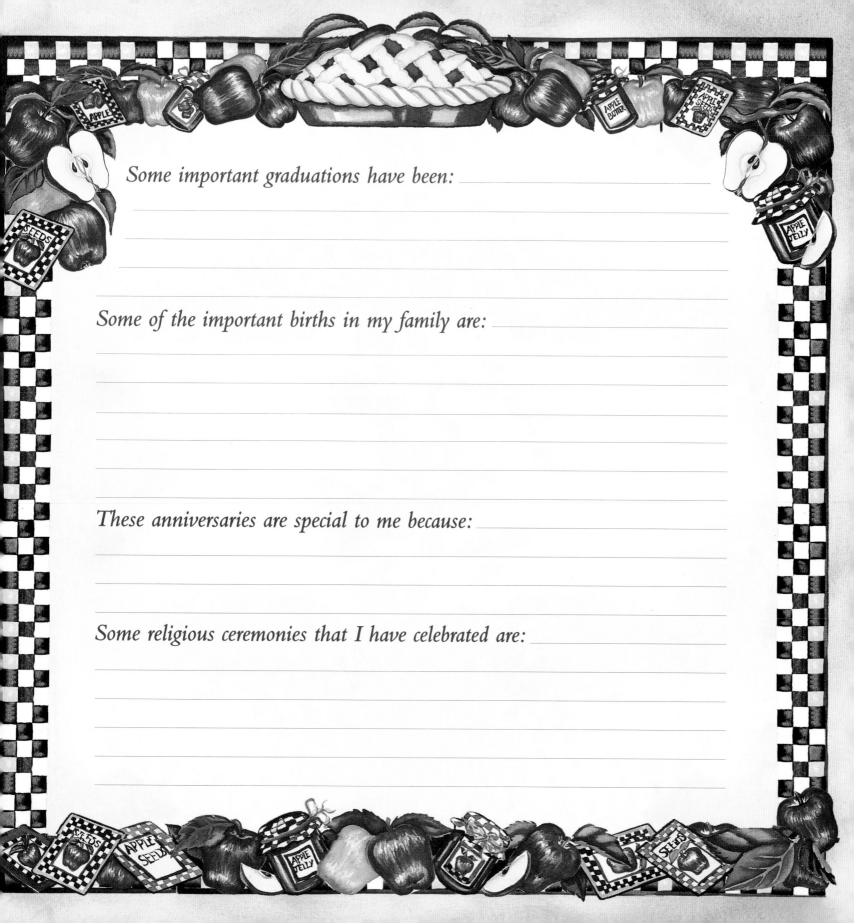

Some important graduations have been: _____
_____
_____
_____

Some of the important births in my family are: _____
_____
_____
_____
_____
_____
_____
_____

These anniversaries are special to me because: _____
_____
_____
_____

Some religious ceremonies that I have celebrated are: _____
_____
_____
_____
_____

Photographs

Photographs

A Few Of My Favorite Things

Some of my favorite movies are: _____

_____

_____

_____

_____

_____

My favorite books and authors are: _____

_____

_____

_____

_____

Some of my favorite music and songs are: _____

Some Memorable Milestones

I remember this about becoming a teenager: _____

_____

_____

_____

_____

_____

_____

My most important birthdays have been: _____

_____

_____

_____

_____

_____

_____

_____

_____

_____

_____

This is what I remember about learning to drive: _____

_____

_____

_____

_____

_____

The celebration of graduating from school was fun because: _____

_____

_____

_____

_____

_____

Coming of age was important because: _____

_____

_____

_____

_____

I Am Proud Of Me

I am most proud of myself because: _____

_____

_____

_____

_____

_____

Remembering the moments that make me proud of who I am: _____

_____

_____

_____

_____

Laurie Korsgaden ©

Photographs

Photographs

Remembering Rainy Days

My favorite rainy day story is about: _____

_____

_____

_____

_____

My favorite things to do on rainy days are: _____

_____

_____

_____

_____

_____

In And Out Of Style

Fashions that were in style that I remember: _____

_____

_____

_____

_____

_____

_____

Some of the popular fashions that I wore were: _____

_____

_____

_____

_____

_____

How my style has changed over the years: _____

_____

_____

_____

_____

It's Time For Spring

My favorite memories of springtime are:

This is what I remember about spring breaks from school:

Something I remember to do every spring is:

Spring is a renaissance for me each year because:

My favorite summertime memories are about:_____

_____

_____

_____

_____

The best summer vacation I have taken has been to:_____

_____

_____

Press Flowers and Leaves here

Remembering Fall

My favorite holidays in fall are: _____

_____

_____

_____

_____

_____

Some fun back-to-school memories are about: _____

_____

_____

_____

_____

_____

_____

_____

Staying Warm In Winter

Some of my favorite memories of winter are about: _____

_____

_____

_____

_____

_____

_____

I remember this about winter breaks from school: _____

_____

_____

_____

_____

_____

Some of the winter sports and activities I enjoy are: _____

_____

_____

_____

_____

_____

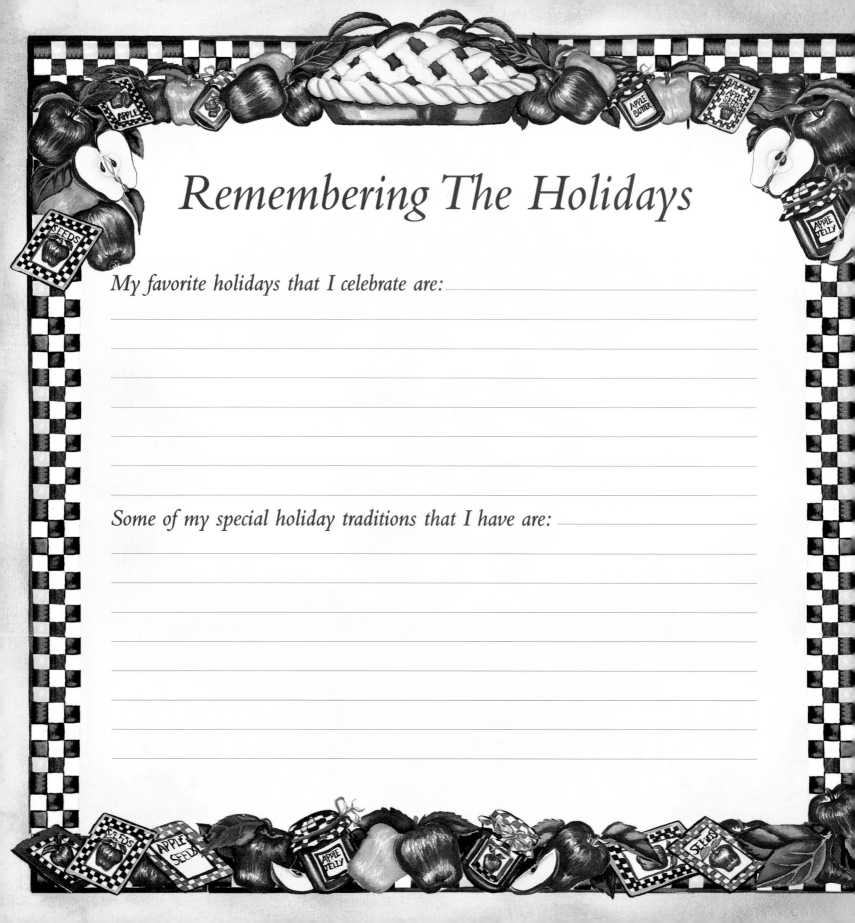

Remembering The Holidays

My favorite holidays that I celebrate are: _____

_____

_____

_____

_____

_____

_____

Some of my special holiday traditions that I have are: _____

_____

_____

_____

_____

_____

_____

_____

During the holidays I often travel to: _____

These are some special memories of holiday celebrations: _____

Attach Keepsakes Here

Attach Keepsakes Here

Remembering My Romances

The most romantic dates that I have had are: _____

_____

_____

_____

_____

_____

_____

The most romantic getaways I have enjoyed are: _____

_____

_____

_____

_____

_____

These are some stories about great romances that I have had: _____

_____

_____

_____

_____

_____

_____

_____

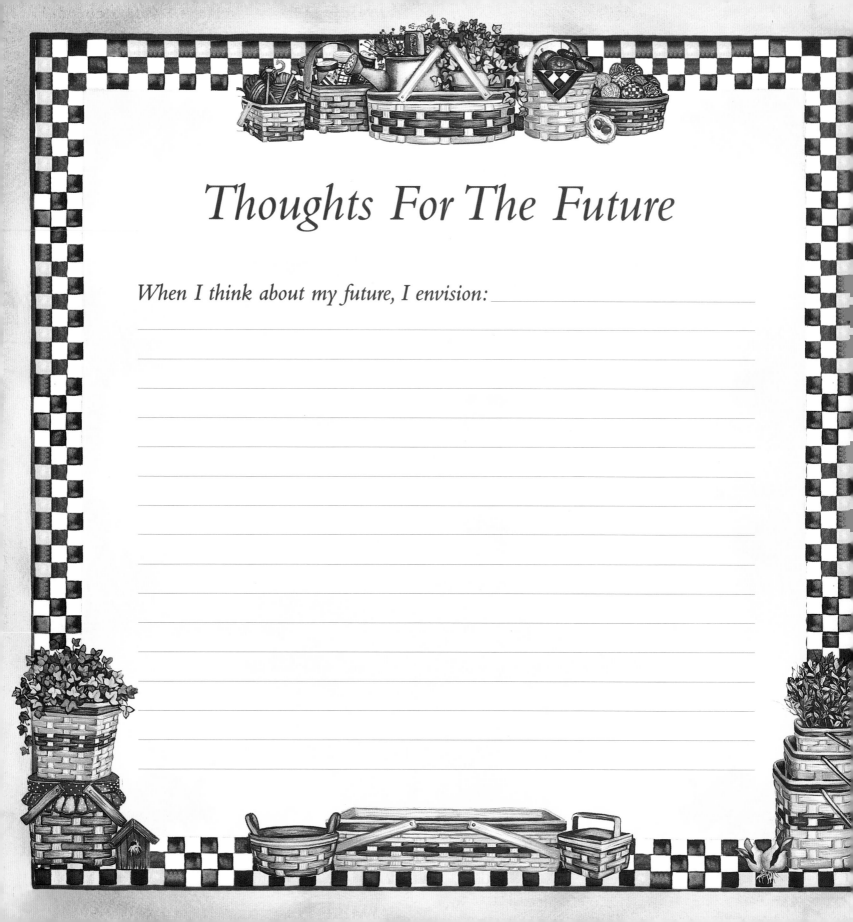

Thoughts For The Future

When I think about my future, I envision: _____

Available Record Books from Havoc

A Celebration of Memories	*Grandparents*
A Circle of Love	*Heart to Heart*
Baby	*It's All About Me!*
College Life	*Mom*
Couples	*Mothers & Daughters*
Family	*My Pregnancy*
Forever Friends	*Our Honeymoon*
Generations	*School Days*
Girlfriends	*Sisters*
Grandmother	*Tying the Knot*

Havoc® PUBLISHING